button girl

More Than 20 Cute-as-a-Button Projects

By Mikyla Bruder
Photographs by Scott Nobles

chronicle books · san francisco

For my dad, with lots of love

Big thanks to the brilliant team at Chronicle, especially Victoria Rock, Susan Zingraf, Beth Weber, Kristen Nobles, and Sara Gillingham. Special thanks also to Brenda Modliszewski (www.bmodjewelry.com) for contributing her button necklace design.

Photographs © 2005 by Scott Nobles.
Illustrations © 2005 by Anne Keenan Higgins.

Book design by Julie Cristello.
Typeset in Memimas, Meta, and Garamond 3.
Manufactured in China.

Library of Congress Cataloging-in-Publication Data
    Bruder, Mikyla.
    Button girl : more than 20 cute-as-a-button projects /
    by Mikyla Bruder.
    p. cm.
    ISBN 0-8118-4553-2
    1. Button craft. 2. Handicraft for girls. I. Title.
    TT880.B78 2005
    745.5—dc22
    2004008944

Distributed in Canada by Raincoast Books
9050 Shaughnessy Street, Vancouver, British Columbia V6P 6E5

10 9 8 7 6 5 4 3 2 1

Chronicle Books LLC
85 Second Street, San Francisco, California 94105

www.chroniclekids.com

Contents

Introduction

They keep your blouse on, your shorts up, and your coat closed. Patterned or smooth, round or square, unassuming buttons are something we encounter every single day, yet we rarely consider them, except perhaps with frustration if they're hard to pop through their little holes.

But the story behind buttons is long and multifaceted. Primitive Button Girls ingeniously employed everything from thorns to bone bits in the attempt to keep their clothing under control. Over time, buttons evolved into a symbol of status and wealth, and craftspeople of every discipline turned their talents toward creating the most intricate buttons, many worth hundreds or even thousands of dollars in the collector market today.

Clothing has long been an indicator of social standing. For centuries European nobility, for example, displayed their prosperity and status through their buttons, each meticulously handcrafted from precious materials, bedecked with jewels, or painstakingly painted with miniature scenes. Indeed, buttons were so valued that even the lower classes passed their (more ordinary) buttons down through generations. Old worn clothing was discarded only after the buttons had been carefully removed and stored away for future use.

Modern times saw the invention of plastic, and the mass production of simple, colored buttons in this material may be the reason behind the button's current reputation as commonplace. Yet today, even the most lackluster of buttons can be surprisingly dear. A new set of buttons for your shirt will set you back more than a few pennies, and decorative buttons for your coat may demand the entire contents of your piggy bank.

A trip to your local fabric store will quickly show that buttons now come in an eye-popping array of colors and designs. Covered in fabric, mass-produced in bright candy shades, or meticulously handcrafted from wood, pearl, gems, metal, glass, or bone, there is a button for every occasion and price range, and then some.

For aspiring Button Girls intrigued by the beauty and bounty of the button, this book offers inspiration and instruction. *Button Girl* kicks off with Button Tips and Techniques, which will teach you everything you'll need to know about buttons for these crafts. The first chapter, Fashion Fun, suggests plenty of ways to give your everyday buttoned-up look a little lift. The second chapter, Button Bijoux, focuses on accessories, with fabulous projects from barrettes to earrings. Chapter 3, Great Gifts, sets out crafty ideas for making delightfully giveable items you'll want to keep for yourself!

So, Button Girl, ransack that junk drawer and that sewing basket, browse the button display in your fabric shop, and scour nearby garage sales, flea markets, and craft emporiums. Start your own button collection and begin putting them to creative use with the project ideas in this book. Isn't it time to return the button to its place of prominence? Let's get started!

Button Tips & Techniques

For button beginners, here is a little information on the types of buttons out there, plus some instructions on the best way to sew them on.

Buttons are generally one of the following types:

• **Sew-through:** These flat buttons have 2 or 4 holes, or "eyes," to accommodate needle and thread.

• **Shank:** These buttons have no visible holes in the top, but they have a small "shank," or loop, on the underside.

• **Ball:** These ball-shaped buttons have a hole drilled through them.

Sewing how-to's:

Flat, 4-eye sew-through button:
Insert the needle through your fabric and one eye from back to front. Find the hole diagonally across from the first hole and insert the needle through that hole and through fabric from front to back. Pull until secure but not tight. Repeat several times. Now insert the needle through one of the two empty buttonholes from back to front, and down through the second empty buttonhole from front to back. This stitch forms a small cross at the top of your button. Repeat several times.

Flat, 2-eye sew-through button:
Use the same technique described for a 4-eye sew-through button without the diagonal crossover.

Shank or ball button: Insert the needle through the fabric from back to front, then through the shank or ball opening, and then back into the fabric near where you began, from front to back. Pull until secure, but not tight. Repeat several times.

If your thread pulls through the fabric, double the knot. When you're attaching a button, keep your stitches small and even, but not too tight. You want the button to be securely attached to the fabric, but you don't want the fabric to gather up around the button. Once your button is attached, always end with your thread on the wrong side of the fabric. Make 3 small stitches, one on top of the other, underneath the stitches you made to attach the button. These 3 stitches work just like a knot, and will help keep your button from coming off. Snip the threads, as closely as possible.

Chapter 1
Fashion Fun

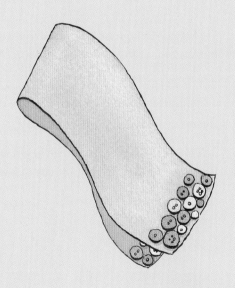

Basic Button Makeover

- 1 button-up blouse or cardigan sweater
- Tape measure or ruler
- Replacement buttons (size, type, and quantity to depend on the shirt)
- Small sewing scissors or stitch ripper
- Needle and thread

Feeling like that button-up top is a bit too, well, buttoned-up? Here's the good news: giving that boring old blouse a makeover is as simple as swapping out its buttons. It's also a great way to practice your button-sewing technique. If you are using sew-through buttons, try using a contrasting color of thread for even more pop.

- - - - -

1. First, examine the current buttons on your shirt or sweater. Measure the diameter of your buttons and purchase a new set in the same size. If you like, clip one off and take it to the store so you can be certain you're buying the right size. All button types are interchangeable for this project, and swapping your plain 2-eye sew-through buttons for sparkly candy-colored shank buttons, for example, is what makes a shirt makeover fun.

2. Use the scissors or stitch ripper to carefully cut the stitching underneath your old buttons. Remove the buttons and excess threads.

3. Thread the needle, aligning the thread ends and tying them together in a knot to double your thread.

4. Now you're ready to attach your new buttons! (Follow the instructions on page 6.)

Blooming Buttons

- Fabric pen
- Skirt, pants, or shirt with humdrum hem(s) or seams
- Flower-shaped buttons
- Needle and embroidery thread in the color of your buttons and in green
- Leaf-shaped beads or buttons (optional)
- Scissors

1

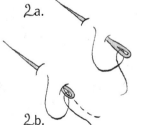

2a.

2b.

A simple change of buttons is nice, but consider this: a button can go anywhere, not just through a buttonhole. If you're feeling like your hems or seams are a little humdrum, add some flower buttons—you can even add a bit of stem and leaf embroidery. The hem and seams of your skirt or dress, the cuffs of your pants, and the pockets of your jeans are all perfect spots for a little flower accent. A bead or button in the shape of a leaf and some green embroidery thread are all it takes to set your petals apart.

- - - - -

1. Pick a spot to embellish. Using the fabric pen, draw 2 slightly curved stems (see illustration 1), then attach buttons at the top of the stems using the needle and thread.

2. Embroider the stems from front to back by backstitching along the pen lines. To backstitch, insert your needle through the fabric back to front about ¼ inch above the bottom of the stem. Then insert your needle through the fabric at the very bottom of the stem front to back. Now, insert your needle up through the fabric from back to front about ¼ inch beyond your needle's first entry point (see illustration 2a). Repeat to create a continuous line of small stitches (see illustration 2b). Knot thread end close to the underside of fabric and snip excess.

3. Embroider leaf shapes or attach leaf-shaped beads or buttons alongside (see illustration 1).

4. Repeat the motif as desired, or create your own pattern for nosegays, bouquets, or even an entire garden in bloom!

Variations: Plain red buttons become cherries dangling from stems and leaves, and a cluster of purple ball buttons can look like a bunch of grapes.

Little Miss Fancy Buttons

- 1 package of cover buttons (available in fabric stores)
- Scissors
- Fabric scraps in light cotton, linen, or silk (nothing thick or stiff)

For variation:
- Lightweight, decorative paper
- Craft glue

Sometimes you just can't find the perfect button. That's when it's time to create your own! Fabric stores carry blank metal buttons specifically designed to be covered with fabric of your own choosing. In selecting your fabric, experiment with texture and pattern, keeping in mind the button's small surface area. Vibrant colors and miniature patterns will show up best. When you're working with patterned fabric, such as a floral print, find and cut out the parts of the pattern that will look nice on the button.

- - - - -

1. On the back of the button package, you will find a circle pattern that you can use to cut fabric circles of the appropriate size to cover your buttons. Cut the pattern out and use it as a template to cut circles from your fabric scraps.

2. Center and stretch a fabric circle over the top of the metal button and hook the fabric onto the teeth just underneath the rim of the button. Once you have all the fabric edges hooked under the button, snap the back plate onto the underside of the button.

Variation: You can also use paper to cover your buttons! Choose a lightweight, interesting-looking paper like rice paper, origami paper, or even newsprint. Cut a circle of paper and coat the underside with a thin, even layer of craft glue. Center the paper over the metal button top and wrap the paper edge under the button. Snip off any long ends and snap on the back plate.

Hip Ribbon Belt

- Pinking shears
- Grosgrain ribbon, 1½ inch wide and long enough to wrap around your waist with 8 inches to spare
- Two 1¾-inch D-rings (available at craft, sewing, and hardware stores)
- Straight pin
- Needle (or sewing machine) and thread
- Fabric pen
- Assorted sew-through buttons

For variation:
- 1 premade ribbon belt

Makes 1 belt

You can use grosgrain ribbon and a couple of D-rings to make a great summer belt. Stitch on a few buttons, and you'll have your very own hip couture. Look for sturdy grosgrain ribbon in a brightly colored stripe or other pattern. For an extra-sturdy belt, sew 2 lengths of grosgrain together for double thickness before proceeding with the instructions.

– – – – –

1. Use the pinking shears to trim one end of the ribbon.

2. Loop the trimmed end of the ribbon through both D-rings (see illustration). Pin down the trimmed end, snugly encasing the straight edges of the D-rings in the ribbon fold.

3. Use the needle or sewing machine to securely stitch the trimmed end to the belt.

4. Try on your belt with a pair of jeans. A standard pair of jeans will have 2 belt loops in front, 2 on the sides, and 1 in the back. You'll want to space your buttons out, stitching buttons between the loops. Using the fabric pen, mark the spots where your buttons will go, spacing them out evenly between the loops. Remove the belt.

5. With the needle and thread, stitch the buttons to the belt at the marked spots.

6. Trim the free end of your belt with the pinking shears, fold the edge ¼ inch under, and stitch along the fold with the needle or sewing machine.

Variation: For a belt that's truly a cinch, decorate a store-bought ribbon belt in the same manner to give it your own special button style.

Snuggly Scarf with Button Trim

You will need:

- Sewing scissors
- Darning needle and finger-weight yarn
- One 7-by-48-inch piece of heavyweight fleece
- Flat, 2-hole sew-through buttons, in an assortment of colors and sizes

For variation:
- Organza ribbon

Makes 1 scarf

Heavyweight fleece is a fun fabric to craft with. It comes in plenty of bright colors, and you can create a simple scarf without the fuss of hemming the edges. In this project, the buttons aren't so much sewn on as they are tied on. The needle carries the sturdy yarn through the fabric and the buttonholes, but you use your fingers to tie the knot on the back side. If you knit or crochet, consider whipping up your own yarn creation and then adorning it with buttons as directed in this project.

- - - - -

1. Cut a 6-inch length of yarn and thread the needle. Bring the needle up through the fleece, leaving 2 inches of yarn on the other side. Taking a button, insert the needle up through one buttonhole and down through the other, then push the needle back through the fleece right beside your first stitch. You now have 2 yarn ends on one side of the fleece, and a button on the other. Tie the yarn ends in a knot and snip excess yarn, leaving ½-inch ends for decoration.

2. Repeat step 1, sewing and tying on additional buttons. You can attach them in a random design, or create a more graphic polka dot or striped pattern. Knot the yarn ends securely on the unbuttoned side of the fleece and snip excess.

Variation: Substitute organza ribbon for the yarn and tie the ribbon ends into bows, for a buttons-and-bows effect. For a super-fast snuggly, hot glue the buttons onto the fabric.

Slumber Party Slippers

- Needle and thread
- 1 pair of fuzzy slippers
- Shank buttons, in an assortment of colors, shapes, and sizes

For variation:

- 1 pair of flip-flops with fabric thongs
- Flat sew-through buttons, in an assortment of colors, shapes, and sizes

Makes 1 pair of slippers

The next time you have a birthday party, entertain your friends by having a fuzzy-slipper slumber party! Provide a pair of slippers for each guest and set out a table full of birthday-themed buttons, needles, and thread. Your pals will stay up late adorning their very own evening footwear. You can even go for a slumber theme with shank buttons in the shapes of cookies and milk, or moons and stars.

- - - - -

1. Thread the needle and knot the ends together to double the thread.

2. Reach inside a slipper with the needle and insert it up through the top of the slipper, pulling it through the other side.

3. Insert the needle through the shank of a button, then push the needle back down through the top of your slipper in the same spot, reaching inside the slipper to pull the needle and thread taut. Repeat several times until the button is secure.

4. Repeat steps 2 and 3, sewing more buttons on the top of the slipper. You can group the buttons in clusters or space them out for a polka dot effect.

5. Repeat the process for the other slipper.

Variation: Dress up your summer flip-flops with assorted sew-through buttons. Look for flip-flops with stitchable fabric thongs and take those buttons to the beach!

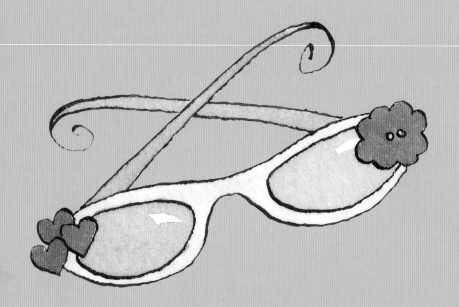

Chapter 2
Button Bijoux

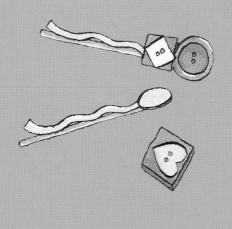

Peony Pin

- One T-shirt
- Scissors
- Photocopy of flower templates on page 59
- Straight pins
- One 1-inch flat sew-through button
- Needle and colored thread
- Metal pin backing (available at fabric and craft stores)

Makes 1 pin

The petals of this pretty peony are made from old T-shirts. T-shirts with a heftier weave will work better than those that are whisper-thin, and colored T-shirts will make your flower even prettier. If you don't want to sacrifice your T-shirts for the cause, you can use scraps of wool or felt instead. Choose a big colorful button for your flower center. The resulting flower makes a versatile accessory and can be pinned to nearly anything—jacket, purse, hat, or backpack.

- - - - -

1. Cut the T-shirt up one side seam and across the top, and open up flat.

2. Cut out the flower patterns and pin to a flat area of the T-shirt. Cut around the flower patterns.

3. Place the smaller flower shape on top of the larger one, and line them up so that the petals look good to you. Sew the button to the flower center, stitching through both layers of fabric.

4. Stitch the pin backing to the back of the flower at its center.

Button Ring

- Ring blank (available at craft and jewelry supply stores)
- Sandpaper
- Glue gun or bead glue
- Flat button (either sew-through or shank button with the shank removed)

Makes 1 ring

Some buttons are as pretty as diamonds, and they're certainly far less expensive! Empy your button drawer and look for unusually pretty buttons to put front and center in this simple project that really showcases a button's beauty. It's the perfect way to use that single button that's lost its mates. Make a different ring for every finger!

- - - - -

1. Some ring blanks have a small platform for easy gluing, and others are just ring-shaped. If yours has a platform, scrub the platform with the sandpaper to achieve a slightly rough surface. If your ring blank doesn't have a platform, decide where on the ring you want the button to go, and scrub that spot with the sandpaper. Scrub the back of your button with the sandpaper to roughen up that surface as well. This will help the glue to adhere better.

2. Apply a dab of glue to the ring blank and carefully place your button onto the glue. Let dry thoroughly before wearing.

Chic Change Purse

- Pinking shears
- One 4-by-8-inch (or larger) sheet of colored craft plastic
- Straight pins
- Embroidery needle and embroidery thread, in contrasting color
- Self-healing craft mat or cutting board
- Utility knife
- One 1-inch button, in same color as embroidery thread

For variation:
- One 4-by-8-inch (or larger) rectangle of colorful oilcloth

Makes 1 change purse

Craft plastic comes in an assortment of candy colors, and can be found at craft and fabric stores. Because it sews up just like fabric and won't unravel at the edges, it's the perfect material for this adorable change purse with button closure.

- - - - -

1. Use the pinking shears to cut a 3½-by-7-inch rectangle of craft plastic. Fold the rectangle as shown in the illustration and pin closed.

2. Using the embroidery needle and thread, stitch along the sides, as indicated by the dotted lines in the illustration.

3. Place the purse on the mat and use the utility knife to carefully cut a 1-inch slit in the flap, as indicated by the straight line in the illustration.

4. Close the flap and push a pin through the center of the slit into the purse. Open the flap, leaving the pin in place. The pin marks the spot where you will attach your button.

5. Remove the pin and stitch the button to the front of the change purse. Fold the flap down and button it closed.

Variation: Use colorful patterned oilcloth instead of craft plastic to create an entirely different look.

Button-Rimmed Sunglasses

You will need:

- Shank buttons in interesting shapes (see note at right)
- Plastic sunglasses, preferably with a cat-eye frame, cleaned and dried
- Wire cutters
- Adult to help
- Metal file
- Glue gun

Makes 1 pair of sunglasses

Shank buttons come in all kinds of interesting shapes: hearts, ice cream cones, sunflowers, and bicycles, to name a few. But that shank on the back—so handy when you're sewing a button onto a shirt—can be very pesky when you're trying to glue the button to a flat surface. Not to worry! The shank can be (very carefully) removed with wire cutters or a utility knife. You must get an adult to help you with this, as gripping the button and cutting off the shank can be tricky. (Note: If you'd rather not bother, just substitute flat sew-through buttons.)

- - - - -

1. Hold up various buttons to the glasses and decide which ones you want to use.

2. Using the wire cutters, with the help of your adult, remove the shanks from the backs of the buttons. You'll want a clean cut, so the backs are nice and flat. File down any remaining portions of the shanks with the metal file.

3. Using the glue gun, attach the buttons to the top outer corners of the sunglasses. Let dry.

Simplest Button Barrette

You will need:

- Measuring tape or ruler
- Scissors
- Ribbon, in a larger width than the barrette
- 1 flat metal or plastic barrette, cleaned and dried
- Glue gun
- Flat sew-through buttons
- Tiny flat-backed rhinestones (optional; available at craft and fabric stores)

For variation:
- Plastic headband

Makes 1 barrette

A plain old barrette gets a chic makeover with ribbon and colorful buttons in different shapes. If you like, add a little extra sparkle with tiny rhinestones.

- - - - -

1. Measure and cut a piece of ribbon the same length as the barrette, then glue it neatly on top. Allow to dry.

2. Now glue the buttons to the top of the ribbon. You can glue them in a tidy row, or pile them high, overlapping and squeezing buttons of all sizes into every corner—it's up to you!

3. If you like, glue rhinestones here and there for extra twinkle.

Variation: To create a button tiara, decorate a plastic headband in the same manner.

Button Bobbies

Just like buttons, bobby pins generally keep a low profile. They do the hard work of keeping those stray, wispy hairs out of your eyes, but they don't have the presence of, say, a sparkly barrette or clip. Brighten up your bobbies and put them front and center with this instant-gratification project. In your craft store, look for special craft bobby pins—these come complete with little metal platforms or pads for gluing on buttons, beads, or flowers (see illustration).

- - - - -

Glue a button to the pad of each bobby pin. You can use 1 button per pin, or stack them, gluing one on top of another for more dimension and color.

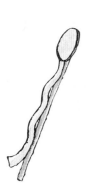

Candy Stripe Earrings

- Two 12-inch pieces 34-gauge silver beading wire
- 8 flat, 2-eye sew-through buttons, in pearly white
- 8 flat, 2-eye sew-through buttons, in pearly pink
- Round-nose pliers
- Chain-nose pliers
- Wire cutters
- 2 French earring hooks

Makes 1 pair of earrings

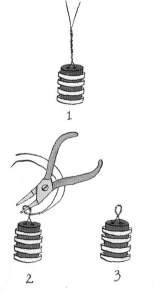

Buttons can be used in the place of beads to make beautiful jewelry. In this project, flat buttons are stacked and attached to French hooks to make pretty, candy-colored earrings. You can find all the tools you need to make them in a bead store.

- - - - -

1. Fold 1 length of wire into a tall skinny U shape, then thread both ends through the eyes of one white button. Follow with a pink button, then a white, and so on, alternating until you have 8 buttons stacked on the wire U. Twist the wire ends tightly, and continue twisting until you have about 1 inch of twisted wire at the top of the button stack (see illustration 1).

2. Using the round-nose pliers, make a small loop in the twisted wire just above the top button (see illustration 2). Grasp the loop firmly with the chain-nose pliers and wrap the twisted wire tail around the base of the loop (just above the top button) several times neatly (see illustration 3). Using the wire cutters, snip off the excess wire, then use the chain-nose pliers to crimp the cut edge of the wire down.

3. Using the chain-nose pliers, open the loop in the French hook. Slip the loop of the button stack onto the loop in the French hook, and close the loop with pliers.

4. Repeat steps 1 through 3 to make the other earring.

Brenda's Button Necklace

You will need:

- 9 inches of 20-gauge metal craft wire
- Chain-nose pliers
- Wire cutters
- 12 inches of 26-gauge metal craft wire
- 4 assorted small to medium buttons (approximately ⅜ inch to ½ inch)
- Silver chain, ribbon, or cord, for hanging the pendant

Makes 1 necklace

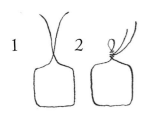

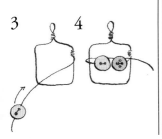

Button Girl at heart, jewelry designer Brenda Modliszewski creates lovely button and bead bangles for her business, bmod jewelry. Here, she shares her method for making a button-and-wire pendant.

- - - - -

1. Bend the 20-gauge wire into a 1-inch square, with the two unfinished ends at the top of the square pointing up (see illustration 1).

2. At the top of the square, pinch the wire ends with two fingers, and use your free hand to curve the ends into a loop about ½ inch above the frame. Grasp the loop with the pliers and use your fingers to wrap the ends around the stem between the loop and the square (see illustration 2). Use the wire cutters to trim the excess wire at the base of the stem, then use the pliers to crimp the cut edge of the wire down. This is the frame of your pendant.

3. Wrap one end of the 26-gauge wire around the top right edge of your frame 4 or 5 times to secure the wire (see illustration 3).

4. Choose a button. Slip the free end of your wire up through a buttonhole from back to front, then down through the second hole from front to back (if the button has 4 holes, use only 2), positioning the button along the wire so it's inside the frame but slightly to the right. Attach a second button in the same fashion, positioning it next to the first.

5. Wrap the wire around the left side of the frame once, then pull it back to the right side, behind the buttons (see illustration 4). Wrap the wire around the right side of the frame, just under the wire you wrapped in step 3. Continue wrapping from the top down, until you reach a good starting

point for your second row of buttons, about two-thirds of the way down the right side of the frame.

6. Repeat step 4, attaching the remaining 2 buttons. Wrap the wire around the left side of the frame once, then pull it back to the right side, behind the buttons. Wrap the wire around the right side of the frame, just under the wire you wrapped in step 4. Wrap 4 to 5 times to secure, use the wire cutters to trim the excess wire at the base of the stem, then use the pliers to crimp the cut edge of the wire down.

7. Hang your pendant from your silver chain, ribbon, or cord as desired.

Chapter 3
Great Gifts

Button Magnets

- Flat sew-through buttons, in an assortment of colors and sizes
- Felt, in assorted colors
- Fabric pen
- Scallop-edged or pinking shears
- Needle and thread, in various colors
- Craft glue
- Round magnets (available at craft stores)

Buttons make the cutest magnets, and plain round magnets are easily found at craft and art supply stores. A "frame" of felt cut with decorative scissors is sandwiched between the button and the magnet, and the result is an adorable little magnet that is perfect for someone's refrigerator or magnet board.

- - - - -

1. Place a button on a piece of felt in a contrasting color and trace around it with the fabric pen. Use the shears to cut around the marked circle, leaving ¼ inch or more to frame the marked circle. Repeat, creating felt "frames" for all of your buttons.

2. Sew the buttons to the centers of their frames on the unmarked side. Knot the threads on the backs of the felt frames on the marked side.

3. Glue the backs of the felt button frames to the magnets. Let dry completely.

Crazy Coasters

- Pinking shears
- One 8½-by-11-inch piece of felt
- One 8½-by-11-inch piece of cork
- Needle and thread
- Flat sew-through buttons galore!
- Craft glue

Makes 4 coasters

The best buttons for this job are flat, and of the same height—shank buttons or ball buttons would make for an uneven coaster! Let loose with different colors, shapes, and sizes of buttons to create an abstract modern look, or go for uniform simplicity and create rows of matching buttons in alternating colors. Cheers!

- - - - -

1. Use the shears to cut the felt and cork into four 4-by-4-inch squares.

2. Thread the needle and knot the ends together to double the thread. Take a felt square and attach the buttons, one at a time, along 1 edge. Continue, filling in the felt square and sewing buttons as closely together as possible, rethreading the needle as necessary, until the entire felt square is covered in buttons. Glue the cork square to the bottom.

3. Repeat step 2 for the remaining 3 squares.

Variation: Feeling like this project is a bit too square? Cut your felt into circles, cloud shapes, flowers, or free-form oblong blobs. There's no rule that says coasters have to be square! Just be sure there's plenty of flat surface area for the base of a glass or a mug.

Nifty Napkin Rings

- Scissors
- 18 inches elastic cord or clear stretchy string (4 pieces, each 4½ inches)
- 1 small binder clip
- Approximately 100 flat sew-through buttons with similar diameters, in an assortment of colors and shapes
- 4 large crimp beads
- Bead cement or good craft glue
- Chain-nose pliers

Makes 4 napkin rings

You can empty your family button drawer for this one, as you'll need about 100 buttons to create all 4 napkin rings. But the resulting project will last a lifetime, and it's a great way to showcase all those odd and forgotten buttons that may never find another use.

- - - - -

1. Cut the elastic in half, and then in half again. You'll have 4 pieces of elastic, each 4½ inches long.

2. Clip the binder clip to the end of one cord length. The clip will prevent the buttons from slipping off the end as you thread them onto the cord.

3. Thread buttons one by one through the elastic so they stack on top of one another. Depending on the thickness of your buttons, you should be able to thread about 25 of them onto the elastic, but feel free to vary the amount as you like.

4. Thread the free end of cord through the crimp bead. Carefully remove the binder clip from the opposite end and thread it through the crimp bead in the opposite direction. Adjust the cord, taking up the slack but being careful not to stretch the elastic. The buttons should line up cozily along the cord with no excess cord between the buttons and the crimp bead.

5. Put a drop of glue inside the crimp bead and use the pliers to smash the crimp. Snip tails and allow glue to dry before using.

6. Repeat steps 1 through 5 to create 3 more napkin rings.

Pretty-as-a-Picture Frame

- 1 small, unfinished-wood picture frame
- Glass cleaner and paper towel
- Flat sew-through buttons, in assorted colors and sizes
- Glue gun
- Photograph to fit frame

For variation:
- Acrylic paint
- Small paintbrush

Makes 1 frame

This button-encrusted frame is a snap to make and a welcome gift—especially with a photo of you inside! A selection of flat buttons in similar hues, such as pinks and reds, or pale blues and greens, makes a standout border for a favorite picture.

- - - - -

1. Remove backing and glass from the frame and wipe the frame free of dirt and dust. Carefully clean the glass.

2. Sort through your buttons, separating the largest buttons in a pile. Beginning with these, attach the buttons to the frame by applying a dab of hot glue onto the frame and then carefully pressing the button into the glue. Glue the large buttons over the frame as close together as possible. Let dry.

3. Using the smaller buttons, fill in the gaps on the frame by applying dabs of hot glue onto the large buttons and carefully pressing the small buttons into the glue. Let dry.

4. Insert your photo into the frame and replace the glass and backing.

Variation: If you prefer a sparser, more graphic design, paint your frame with a vibrant shade of acrylic paint and let dry before decorating with a few well-chosen buttons.

Button Keepers

- Your button collection
- Assorted jars, cleaned and dried
- High-gloss enamel paint, in various colors or just one color, as desired
- Sponge brush
- Craft glue
- Rickrack trim (optional)

A **Button Girl** needs a handy way to organize her button collection. Clean food jars of varying shapes and sizes are the perfect receptacles for a button collection. Organized by color and arranged on a shelf, they're easy to select from and so pretty to look at. Look for interesting jar shapes, like stubby baby-food jars, beveled jam jars, and tall, narrow olive jars.

- - - - -

1. Sort your buttons by color, putting them in piles. Group them as you like, putting all blues together, for example, or separating out different hues.

2. Match the size of the jars to the button piles and fill each jar with its designated button grouping.

3. Working in a well-ventilated space and on a protected work surface, paint the tops and outside rims of the jars. Set on newspaper and let dry.

4. Glue 1 of the buttons from each jar to its respective lid, so you can easily remember which lid belongs on which jar. If you like, glue a length of rickrack trim around the outside rim of the jar lid.

Dressed-up Greeting Cards

- One 8½-by-11-inch sheet card stock, in color and pattern of your choice
- Photocopy of dress template on page 60
- Pencil
- Scissors and scallop-edged or pinking shears
- Craft glue
- 12 small, flat sew-through buttons (about 5/16 inch in diameter)
- 4 glassine envelopes, each 3 by 4 inches
- ⅛-inch, single-hole punch
- Four 6-inch pieces of ½-inch organza ribbon

Makes 4 greeting cards

These cute, frock-shaped greeting cards are easy to make. Try creating cards of a different shape, like coats and shirts, or overalls. Glassine envelopes are see-through envelopes, available at good paper and craft stores. If you can't find them, just substitute plain paper envelopes of a similar size.

- - - - -

1. Fold the card stock in half, lengthwise.

2. Cut out the dress pattern and place it on the far left-hand side of the folded card stock, leaving just enough room for the left sleeve and aligning the dotted neckline along the folded edge. Use the pencil to lightly trace around the pattern.

3. Using straight scissors, cut around all lines except for the bottom hem. Use the scallop-edged or pinking shears to cut along the bottom hem.

4. Repeat steps 2 and 3 three times, each time moving the pattern to the right of the cut area, tracing and cutting 3 more dress shapes, to total 4 cards.

5. Glue 3 small buttons on the front of each paper dress as indicated in the pattern. Let dry.

6. Write your messages inside the cards and slip the cards into the glassine envelopes, pushing them down so the bottom hem touches the bottom of the envelope. Close the envelope flaps and, using the hole punch, punch 2 small holes through the top of each envelope, being careful not to punch through the cards. Thread the ribbon in through 1 hole from front to back, and the other end through the other hole from back to front. Tie the ends together in a knot or small bow. Trim ends if desired.

Cute-as-a-Button Gift Wrap

Buttons make great gifts, but they also make great gift adornments. In this project, we thread buttons onto colored twine to create a pretty gift-wrap string. Then, we use a single button to create a gift tag that tells a friend that this gift is "cute as a button."

- - - - -

1. To make the decorative button twine, first determine how much twine you need by wrapping it around your gift and cutting off the necessary amount. Next, thread buttons onto your twine, spacing the buttons evenly or scrunching them close together as desired. Use all one kind of button, or mix it up for a fun, polka-dot effect. Tie the button twine around your wrapped gift.

2. To make the cute-as-a-button gift tag, use a colorful pen to write the words "Cute as a" on the gift tag. Glue or sew a button underneath the words and use twine or ribbon to attach the gift tag to the gift.

CUTE AS A

Button Print Stationery

- Flat sew-through buttons, in assorted sizes
- Glue gun
- Corks
- Scratch paper
- Magazine
- Colored ink pads
- Blank stationery sheets with matching envelopes
- Silk cord or ribbon

For variation:
- Sponge brush
- Fabric paint
- Fabric items, for stamping

Buttons make great stamps. Different types make different marks, and you can have fun experimenting with shapes and patterns. For your first try, look for a nice flat sew-through button with a little bit of detailing around the edge. (Tip: Don't ignore the backs of the buttons—they often provide a smoother surface.) Try out different designs and use your button stamps to decorate anything from cards to wrapping paper to pillowcases. This stationery makes a lovely gift.

- - - - -

1. Use the glue gun to attach a button to the end of a cork, being careful not to apply too much glue (which can seep through the buttonholes and spoil your print). Let dry. Repeat as desired, making additional button stamps.

2. Place your scratch paper on top of the magazine (the magazine makes a soft surface, which helps you to achieve a better print). Ink your stamps and try them out. Practice making a good impression.

3. Now decorate your stationery using your best stamps in a pattern of your choosing. Decorate an entire side with a repeating pattern, or just stamp around the edges. Let dry.

4. Stack the stationery and envelopes and tie with a piece of silk cord or ribbon. Thread one cord end through a button and tie the cord to secure.

Variation: Use a sponge brush to coat your button stamps with a thin, even layer of fabric paint and stamp on soft cotton napkins, pillowcases, or clothing. Just be sure to practice first so you know you can make a good impression!

Mini Book

- One 8½-by-11-inch sheet of rice paper or similar lightweight writing paper
- Paper cutter or scissors
- Ruler
- Pencil
- One 8½-by-11-inch sheet patterned card stock
- Cutting board
- Needle and embroidery thread
- 1 flat sew-through button in a special shape

Makes 1 mini book

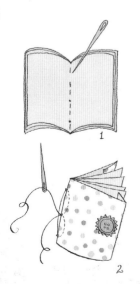

The pages of this miniature book are made from a single sheet of paper. The cover is made from patterned card stock, but feel free to try different heavyweight papers for your book covers. Recycle old greeting cards, postcards, or CD covers for a fun, graphic look. Use your book as a tiny journal, a mini album filled with glued-in photo cutouts, or a small stamp-collecting book.

- - - - -

1. Fold the lightweight sheet of paper in half, widthwise, matching the edges carefully. Open the sheet and cut or tear along the fold. You now have 2 sheets of paper, each 5½ by 8½ inches. Fold these sheets in half again, matching the edges carefully. Open the sheets and cut or tear along the folds. You now have 4 sheets of paper, each 4¼ by 5½ inches. Fold these papers in half, lengthwise, matching the edges carefully. Open them and cut or tear along the folds. You now have 8 sheets of paper, each 2⅛ by 5½ inches. Fold these sheets in half, widthwise. These are the pages of your book: 16 pages, each 2¾ inches wide and 2 inches tall. Set aside.

2. Using the ruler and pencil, outline a long, narrow rectangle on the card stock, 7¾ by 2¼ inches. Cut out the rectangle, then fold it in half, widthwise. Fold 1 inch of each end in as shown (see illustration 2). This is your book cover. The folded ends are called flaps.

3. On the cutting board, unfold the cover and lay it flat. Place your folded pages from step 1 flat on top of the flattened cover, neatly matching up all center creases. Use the needle to make 3 holes along the center crease, carefully poking the needle through all the paper layers, including the inside pages and cover (see illustration 1). Position 1 hole near the top of the center crease, 1 hole near the bottom, and 1 right in the middle.

Tips for tearing paper:
A torn paper edge can look feathery and soft—a nice alternative to a cleanly cut edge. But even when torn, the edge should be straight and neat. Before tearing, be sure to fold the paper very carefully, and crease it well with your fingers or a bone folder (a tool found in craft stores made specifically for paper projects). Then use a damp sponge to lightly moisten the folded edge. Unfold the paper, lay it flat, and place one hand firmly alongside the fold. Use your other hand to slowly tear the paper along the fold.

4. Thread your needle with 18 inches of embroidery thread. Holding the book in one hand, insert your needle through the center hole from the outside of the cover to the inside of the book, and pull until you have about 10 inches of thread remaining on the outside of the book. Insert your needle through the top hole from the inside of the book and pull the thread taut, still leaving about 10 inches of thread on the outside of the book at the center hole. Now insert your needle through the bottom hole from the outside in, and then back through the center hole from the inside out (see illustration 2). Pull both thread ends to tighten your stitches, and tie the ends in a knot just over the center hole. Trim ends to about 9 inches long.

5. Sew the button to the front of the book, stitching through the front cover only, not the flap. The flap will conceal the stitches on the inside cover. Close the book and wrap the thread ends from the spine of the book around the back of the book and then forward around the button to secure.

Templates

For "Peony Pin," page 22

bottom

top

For "Dressed-up Greeting Cards," page 50